The Marble Palace, built 1787–1791 in Potsdam, was the preferred summer residence of the Prussian king Frederick William II (1744–1797). In 1783, when he was crown prince, Frederick William had purchased a simple summer home on the shore of the Heiliger See. One year after his coronation, he had the architect Carl von Gontard (1731–1791) start on the construction of a two-story villa, with brick masonry in the Dutch style and sidings of Silesian marble. It was crowned with a belvedere that offered a wide view of what at that time was a landscape of lakes still unblemished by other buildings. The Marble Palace was

Page 1:
Marble Palace,
side view with
kitchen

the first royal palace in Prussia built in the Classical style, which replaced Frederician Rococo after Frederick II's death in 1786.

In 1790, the interior design was delegated to Carl Gotthard Langhans (1732–1808), who was at that time just completing the construction of the Brandenburg Gate in Berlin. Many of the Berlin and Potsdam artists and craftsmen called into service for the new palace had previously collaborated in the building of the Frederician palaces, and now found themselves in the position of having to work in the Classical style. Baron Friedrich Wilhelm von Erdmannsdorff (1736–1800), journeyed to Italy to acquire Antique sculptures and Classicist marble fireplaces for the furnishing of the Marble Palace and other palaces of the king. As decorations for the fireplace mantels, the king ordered the purchase of Antique-style vases from Josiah Wedgwood (1730–1795).

A few years after its completion, the palace was enlarged. Since by now the king was having difficulty going up and down steps, the architect Michael Philipp Boumann (the younger) (1747–1803) added two one-story side wings in 1797. The health of the king necessitated a rapid implementation of the project but it was not possible to come by the Silesian marble quickly enough. Instead, the Rehgarten Colonnade from the park of Sanssouci was torn down and the marble from its columns was used for the new colonnades. When, on 16 November 1797, the king passed away in the Marble Palace, the side wings were still under construction. The interior decoration was not carried out until 1843–1848, under the orders of Frederick William IV (1795–1861), by Ludwig Ferdinand Hesse (1795–1876). The work was finally completed with the painting of the colonnades, which depicted scenes from the Song of the Nibelungen. However, the palace was never again used by the king himself, but rather by various members of

Anonymous artist, view of the garden side, around 1789

3

the royal household, who made use of the side wings as their annual summer residence.

The main building was reserved for future imperial couples. From 1831 to 1835, Prince William of Prussia, the future Emperor William I (1797–1888), and Augusta, née Princess of Saxony-Weimar-Eisenach (1811–1890), resided there. In 1881, the upper floor was renovated – "with great respect for the previous décor" – to create a summer apartment for Prince William of Prussia, the future Emperor William II (1859–1941), and Auguste Victoria, née Princess of Schleswig-Holstein-Sonderburg-Augustenburg (1858–1921). From 1904 to 1917, Crown Prince William of Prussia (1882–1951) and Cecilie, Duchess of Mecklenburg-Schwerin, lived here.

After the end of the monarchy, the sanitary facilities and the heating fixtures originating in imperial times were removed. The rooms, now accessible to the public, were provided with their original eighteenth-century furnishings. During the Second World War, the main building was damaged by grenades and the northern wing by fire bombs. After 1945, Soviet officers used the palace as a casino for several years. From 1961 to 1989, it served as a military museum for the German Democratic Republic. The extensive renovation begun in 1988 was continued by the State Palaces Administration in 1990 and was completed in 2004 with the interior decoration. All of the Marble Palace rooms have once again been open to the public since 2006.

So that the room descriptions are easy to find as the tour progresses, the rooms have been ordered according to the numbers designated in the floor plan.

Main Building

Vestibule and Stairway (Rooms 13 and 14)

Four decoratively veined monolithic marble columns from Silesia separate the vestibule and the stairway. The floors, skirting boards, and pedestals are also faced with Silesian marble. The cast iron grids set into the floor are part of the central heating system that was installed in 1881. The walls of the vestibule are decorated with green plaster porphyry and plaster Tuscan pilasters. The Potsdam plasterer Constantin Sartori (1747–ca. 1812) carried out the plastering of the ceiling and the overdoors. The only one of the Marble Palace's early Classical light fixtures that has been completely preserved is the lantern in the vestibule. The antique **marble sculpture** of Oenone (2nd c. CE) came into the Berlin Antiquities Collection in 1830 and from there it returned to its original display location in 2006. The **marble vases,** crafted in Italy around 1795, originally flanked the entrance portal on its outer side.

The mirrored dining room with its two flanking preparation rooms is connected by a subterranean passageway to the palace kitchen at the lakeshore (Temple Ruin). The dining room's location directly at the water and the walls' marble sidings ensured a pleasantly cool room temperature in the summer. In 1790/1791 this room was redesigned as a grotto, in accordance with Antique and Baroque traditions; Sartori supplied pilasters featuring Hermes and lacquered plaster seashells. The **ceiling paint-**

Grotto Hall

◁ Upper floor,
view towards
the ceiling

ing, carried out in 1793 by Christian Bernhard Rode (1725–1797), shows Poseidon kidnapping the nymph Amphitrite. Further scenes are populated by nymphs and other inhabitants of the seas. The Antique **marble sculpture** of the nymph Thetis has been returned to the grotto-style hall from the Berlin Collection of Classical Antiquities. The six **chairs** (ca. 1793) are originally from the Gothic Library, and the eight **stools** (ca. 1791) are from the Orangery in the New Garden.

Conversation Room (White Lacquer Chamber) (Room 16)

Wilhelmine Ritz (the future Countess Lichtenau) commissioned Johann Carl Wilhelm Rosenberg (1725–

7

1797) to fit this chamber with white lacquer wood panelling and painted grape-leaf borders. After 1881, the room served as the adjutant's chamber. The ceiling painting was destroyed in 1945 and the painted ceiling decorations were renovated in 1954. In 1954 and 1997, the partially surviving panelling was completed. The reconstruction of the veneered boarded parquet flooring took place in 1997. The **set of Wedgwood vases for the chimneypiece**, a **fireplace screen** by Johann Ephraim Eben (1748–1805), two **cabinets** by David Hacker (1748–1801), six **armchairs** designed by Langhans, as well as a **grandfather clock** with a Glockenspiel (Paris, 1751–1756) all belong to the original furnishings (ca. 1790/91). The **pastel portraits** which now supplement the original décor show Frederick William II, his wife, and his children.

Conversation Room, White Lacquer Chamber

Music Room

Music Room (Blue Lacquer Chamber)
(Room 17)

Frederick William II, who was an enthusiastic cello player, originally kept his sheet music in the built-in wall cabinet behind the lacquered panelling. After 1881, Prince William (II.) used the space as a living room and later as a reception room. The wall painting, which was carried out in 1790 by Rosenberg after Langhans' design has only survived in fragments. The Antique-style tripods and musical instruments refer to Apollo as the guardian of the muses. The ceiling painting, "Gardening, Hunting, and Fishing", was destroyed. The reconstruction of the decorative painting of the ceiling took place in 1954. In 1997, the veneered boarded parquet was reconstructed,

using original parquet boards. The **marble fireplace** by Carlo Albaccini, the **set of chimneypiece vases** by Wedgwood, a **fireplace screen**, two **cabinets** by Hacker, six **armchairs**, and a **sofa** belong to the original furnishings (ca. 1790/91). The two Roman portraits of youths, once thought to be likenesses of Gaius and Lucius Caesar, have come back to the palace from the Berlin Collection of Classical Antiquities.

Boiseried Writing Room (Room 19)

In this corner cabinet, used as a "writing chamber", Frederick William II passed away in 1797 after a prolonged illness. After 1881, the room was the study of Prince William (II.) The veneered panelling of taxus, walnut, mulberry, maple, and fruit trees was crafted in 1790, after designs by Langhans. The meander decoration refers to the recently (18th c.) discovered Greek origin of Antique art. The **dragon head** next to the door was removed from the Potsdam City Palace in 1791 and used as a warm air vent for the oven in the cellar. The ceiling painting was restored in 1954, after a fire. The reconstruction of the parquet floor, the mirror frame, and the overdoor followed in 1996/97. The original furnishings include the **wall table** with its precious marble plate, the **bronze statuette** of a landing Nike on a marble sphere, and the Roman **funeral urn** (from the Collection of Classical Antiquities).

Yellow Writing Room (Room 20)

After 1881, the workroom of Frederick William II served as a vestibule for a royal guest apartment. The ceiling painting, carried out in 1790/93, the mirror frame, and the overdoor refer to Wisdom, the virtue pertaining to a good ruler. In the **ceiling painting**, Rode depicted Minerva, the goddess of wisdom, promising the young ruler honour and fame. Frisch painted a homage to the Three Graces for the **overdoor**. The plaster putti of the fireplace mirror, created by Sartori in 1791, hold a mirror and a snake in their hands as an attribute of Wisdom. The parquet floor, the mirror frame, and the English steel fireplace are originals. The silk wall covering and the woven border of roses were reconstructed in 1997. The original furnishings (ca. 1790/91) included the **wall table** with the marble plate, the four **armchairs**, the **fireplace screen**, as well as a **clock** with a mechanical calendar and Glockenspiel from the estate of Madame Pompa-

Yellow Writing Room

dour (1737/57). The Roman funeral urn has been returned to the Writing Room from the Berlin Collection of Classical Antiquities. Four **gouaches** with Pompeiian dancers replace the lost series of engravings of views of the Vatican loggias by Giovanni Volpato. The **portrait** by Anton Graff (1736–1813) depicts Princess Friederike (1767–1820), the oldest daughter of the king.

Dressing Room, Green Chamber
(Room 21)

After 1881, Frederick William's dressing room served as the living room of the royal guest apartment. The 1793 **ceiling painting** by Frisch shows Hebe and Amor on Mount Olympus. The parquet floor, the panels,

Dressing Room, Green Chamber

and the doors are the originals. The wall covering of green Peking silk, and the arabesque borders and painted overdoors on red Atlas silk, were reconstructed in 1997. Giacomo Rafaelli's **marble fireplace** with its mosaic décor, the **set of Wedgwood vases** on the fireplace mantel, the two **cabinets** by Hacker, a mahogany **fireplace screen**, four **armchairs**, and the intarsia **escritoire** all belong to the original furnishings (1790/91). The Roman **marble bust**, previously "Marciana", went to the Berlin Collection of Classical Antiquities in 1830. The **painting** with the depiction of Frederick William II and his sister as well as the silhouette portraits of the royal family of Prussia and the stadtholder family of Orange supplement the decor.

Sleeping Chamber (Room 23)

After 1881, the king's sleeping chamber served as a bedroom for royal visitors. In 1790, Johann Gottlieb Fiedler (1735–until after 1797), panelled the walls and floor after designs by Langhans to create an "Etrurian" intarsia cabinet made of taxus and other veneer woods. Alongside Greece, Etruria was also considered one of the lands of origin of Classical Antique art. The **ceiling paintings** by Frisch, "Morpheus and the Sleeping Endymion", as well as "Phosphoros" and "Hesperos" (the morning and evening stars) refer to the use of the room. The **cabinet** and the **corner cupboard** by Hacker are from the original furnishings.

Upper Stairway (Room 24)

The upper walls were articulated with plaster Ionic pilasters in 1790 and were decorated with plaster arabesques by Sartori. In 1793, the stage design painter Bartolomeo Verona took over the painting of the stairway dome.

Antechamber (Room 26)

After 1881, the antechamber was changed into a dressing room for Auguste Victoria; after 1945, it was again remodelled. The framed wood panelling, the pillar mirrors of the window wall, and some fragments of the original wall covering have survived. The stripe-patterned silk of the wall covering was reconstructed in 1998 after some original remains. A renovation of the ceiling painting and the parquet floor followed in that same year. The **cabinet** and the **three chairs** (ca. 1790) were previously in other rooms

Sleeping Chamber

of the Marble Palace. The **paintings** depict Frederick
William (II.) as Prince of Prussia (ca. 1785) and his son,
Frederick William (III.) as crown prince.

Antechamber

En Camaieu Chamber
(Room 28)

The cameo-like or stone-cutting-like style in which
the wall was painted gave this room its unusual
name. It was executed in 1790 by Johann Eckstein after a design by Langhans. For the figures and the decorative motifs, Langhans was inspired by the décor
of the loggia walls of the Vatican. The chamber, originally conceived as a living and recreational room,
was used after 1881 by Auguste Victoria and later by
Cecilie as a dressing room.

En Camaieu
Chamber

The ceiling painting, which was destroyed in 1945, and parts of the wall painting were replaced by copies in 1954. The reconstruction of the parquet floor and the fireplace mirror followed in 1999. The **marble fireplace** by Lorenzo Cardelli, the **set of fireplace mantel vases by Wedgwood,** and a **chair** are all part of the original furnishings. The Roman **Priapus Hermes** of marble has come back from the Berlin Collection of Classical Antiquities. Supplementary furnishings are a **cabinet** from the Marble Palace by Eben (ca. 1790), and a **sofa** and a **chair** from the Gothic Library (ca. 1793). The **console table** by Eben (ca. 1796) is from the library of Frederick William II in Charlottenburg Palace.

Brown Room (Room 29)

This room, also called the "Little Hall", was decorated with brown silk in 1790, and served as a bedroom for the royal couples from 1881 onwards. Rosenberg created the ceiling painting with its coffered look and early Classicist decorative motifs. The pillar mirrors and the base panels as well as a few of the panels of the veneered parquet floor of 1790 are still original. The originally decoratively-painted silk wall covering was replaced with simple wallpaper in 1954. The **marble fireplace** by Pietro Finelli, and the fireplace mantel **set of Wedgwood vases** belong to the original furnishings. The **ottomans, chairs,** and **cabinets** were crafted in Berlin in 1790/95 and were previously in Charlottenburg Palace.

Landscape Room (Room 30)

After 1881, the Landscape Room, which had been furnished in 1790/91, was changed into a toilet and dressing chamber for the princes. The walls of the room used to be completely covered with full-sized landscape paintings that have been considered lost since 1950. The mirror frame, the base panels and the wooden wall panelling, parts of the veneered boarded parquet floor, and two painted **overdoors** by J. Grätsch depicting the four seasons have all survived. The ceiling painting has not survived; the decorative painting was reconstructed in 1999. The **fireplace** made of Italian gold-veined marble, the **Wedgwood vase mantelpiece set**, and the Roman **marble sculpture** of the Venus de' Medici from the Berlin Museum of Antiquities have survived. The 1790 **painting** by Rode showing the allegories of the elements – air, fire, water, and earth – originally was used as an overdoor in the apartment of Queen Friederike Luise in the Berlin City Palace. The **cabinet** by Eben and the **game table** were also crafted around 1790, in Berlin.

Oriental Cabinet (Room 31)

Earlier known by the names "Turkish Room", "Tent Room", or "Turkish Tent", this cabinet served Prince William (II.) as a salon after 1881. The tent, which was produced around 1790 after the designs of Langhans, was made of blue and white striped Atlas fabric and of silk with a leopard-skin pattern. It was decorated with ostrich feathers and furnished with a Turkish divan. The room was somewhat reduced in size after 1881 to make possible the construction of a wardrober's chamber directly above it. In the post-war years, the octagonal tent construction was destroyed. The

Concert Hall

two pillar mirrors survived as well as one original parquet board and some fragments of silk. The tent room was reconstructed in 1998/99.

Concert Hall (Room 32)

This hall was originally used for concerts and other festivities; after 1881, it served as a living room and salon. The décor is from 1790, based on the designs of Langhans. The hall extends across the whole width of the main building and offers a view of the water from three sides. The originally bright blue plaster walls, now faded, the plaster Corinthian pillars and the pilasters are the work of Sartori. Johann Gottfried Schadow (1764–1850) created the ten bas-reliefs, of framed blue and white plaster, depicting Antique ritual sacrifice and celebration scenes. The overdoor reliefs, made of white plaster backed by red plaster porphyry, show a proces-

◁ Oriental
Cabinet

21

sion of oceanic beings. The wall and fireplace mirrors have also survived. The ceiling painting was destroyed by fire after 1945, when the roof went up in flames. In 1996/97, a simplified version of the painted coffered ceiling was reconstructed. At its midpoint, the original ceiling showed "Aeneas at the Banks of the Tiber". The boarded parquet, designed by Langhans, with its leafy star-shape at the centre, was reconstructed in 1999 using surviving fragments. The two **marble fireplaces** by Carlo Albaccini, and the two **sets of mantelpiece vases** by Wedgwood belong to the original furnishings, as does also a Roman marble statue of Apollo, which will soon be returned to its original location in the palace from the Berlin Collection of Classical Antiquities. Now standing in its place in the niche is a plaster cast of the so-called "Große Hekulanerin" (large figure from Herculaneum). The **fireplace screens** are from the furnishings of the Marble Palace, and the **chairs** (ca. 1790) presumably from buildings in the New Garden. Two **cabinets** and a pair of **vase candelabras** from Berlin (1790–1800) supplement the original furnishings.

South Wing

The construction of the interior of the South Wing proceeded in 1843/46 under the direction of the architect Ludwig Ferdinand Hesse. Three large state-rooms were located on the side facing the garden, and smaller bedrooms, cavaliers' rooms, and personnel rooms were situated facing inward to the courtyard. The fixed interior décor and the parquet floors were restored and partially extended in 1996. There is very little remaining of the original moveable furnishings. The artworks on display here refer to King Frederick William II himself, his personal circle of friends, and his main apartment in the destroyed Berlin City Palace.

Connecting Gallery (Room 49)

Carl Gotthard Langhans, Concert Hall, design for the boarded parquet floor, 1790

In 1843/45, Bernhard Wilhelm Rosendahl (1804–1846), using the Vatican Loggia as an inspiration, painted the gallery connecting the Main Building and the South Wing. Fifteen picture spaces, after models by Hesse and after other contemporary engravings, display views of Sicily, including Palermo, Agrigento, and Taormina. The marble busts after Antique models – the Diana of Versailles, Menelaus, and the Apollo Belvedere – were crafted in the mid-nineteenth century by August Wredow and Francesco Sanguinetti.

Vestibule (Room 50)

Page 24/25:
Anonymous artist, Potsdam, view across the Heiliger See to the Marble Palace and the kitchen building, around 1793

In the nineteenth century, the floor was laid out with grey and white marble and the walls were painted in an imitation of marble. The painting of the wall was redone in 1996 in observance of recent findings. Around 1790, Eckstein produced the grisaille paintings "Europe" and "Asia" for the belvedere on the roof of the Marble Palace.

Green Room (Room 51)

This room was planned in 1797 as the "Turkish" or "Divan" room, but in 1845 was furnished as an anteroom, and later as a bedroom and a reception room. The oak parquet floor has survived and the green painted walls with gilt skirting boards have been renovated according to the original designs. The figures of children in the ceiling painting by Rosendahl display the various art forms. The **paintings** by Anton Graff, Anna Dorothea Therbusch, and other artists of that epoch depict Frederick William II, Queen Friederike of Prussia, Wilhelmine Encke, Julie Amalie Elisabeth Countess of Ingenheim, and the king's favourite son Alexander von der Mark, who died an early death. A **grandfather clock**, a **cylinder desk**, and a **revolving armchair** by David Roentgen (1743–1807) supplement the original furnishings.

Anna Dorothea
Therbusch,
Wilhelmine Encke,
the later Countess
of Lichtenau,
1776

Purple Salon (Room 52)

In 1797, this room was supposed to be decorated with the landscape paintings which the Countess Lichtenau had acquired in Italy. Around 1845, when used as a living room, the walls were painted purple, the skirting boards were gilt, and it was furnished with a marble fireplace and a boarded parquet floor. The **ceiling painting** by August Kloeber (1793–1864) displays the four seasons in the zodiac. Included in the acquisitions of Countess Lichtenau are the **paintings** of Italian landscapes from Antiquity, and scenes from Classical Antique and Nordic mythology and the Bible. The **furniture** originates in part from the main apartment of Frederick William II. The designs for the rosewood **console table** and the **grandfather clock** crafted by Fiedler and Möllinger probably are the work of the privy counsellor Carl Ludwig Bauer (1750–1808).

Oval Hall (Room 54)

The oval shape of this room was already decided upon in 1797. The pillars, with plaster faux marble, are presumably from the eighteenth century. The capitals, the yellow faux-marble walls, and the green pilasters were constructed in the nineteenth century. After 1881, the room served as a dining or festivities hall. The **ceiling painting** by Heinrich Lengerich, "Helios and Aurora", repeats a famous painting be Guido Reni. The centre of the oak parquet floor displays decorative inlay work of mahogany and maple. The Antique-style **marble fireplace** of Carrara marble and the two **marble sculptures** by Eduard Mayer in the eastern wall niches, the Crouching Venus and the Sandal Fastener, belong to the original furnishings. The two marble figures standing opposite one another, by Edme Bouchardon, the Lamb Bearer and the Faun Playing a Flute, were previously in the king's chambers. The two mahogany **guéridons** with glass pendants, the gilt armchair, and the **throne** belong to the original furnishings from the main apartment of Frederick William II in the Berlin City Palace.

Grandfather clock in the Purple Salon

Oval Hall

Cavalier's Apartment (Rooms 59 and 58)

This apartment, furnished around 1845, was meant for the cavaliers and ladies-in-waiting in the retinue of the prince. In 1882, the lord steward of Prince William (I.) moved into these rooms. The wall paintings in the small bedroom (Room 59) are based on models in Pompeii. Likewise, the living room (Room 58) is painted with "Pompeiian" red, wax-based paint and framed with gilt skirting boards. The fireplace, constructed of different types of stones of various colours and the ceiling paintings of the living room are the original furnishings. The **marble figure** of Hippomenes by Jean-Antoine Tassaert (1727–1728), the **five marble reliefs** by Johann Christian Unger – Apollo, Omphale, Melpomene, Ajax, and Victoria – and the **mahogany door**, crafted after the designs of Erdmannsdorff all come from the royal chambers in the Berlin City Palace.

North Wing

The interior of the North Wing was constructed in 1845–48. Prince Albrecht, the brother of Frederick William IV, and Princess Alexandrine were the first inhabitants in the summer of 1850. In the following years, the nieces and nephews of the childless king used the North Wing as a summer home: Princess Charlotte and Georg (II.), the crown prince of Sachsen-Meiningen from 1850 to 1854, Prince Friedrich Karl and Princess Maria Anna of Anhalt from 1855 to 1880, and Prince Albrecht, Jr. from 1866 to 1872. The furnishings were changed according to the wishes of the respective inhabitants. In 1881, William (II.) and Auguste Victoria had guest apartments built in the North Wing, and in the following year, children's quarters were added. From 1905 to 1917, the children of the last crown princely couple, William and Cecilie, lived in the "Princes' Wing". A fire bomb in 1944, and the renovations for the military museum after 1961, particularly affected the North Wing. In this wing, reconstructed in 2004, the onetime inhabitants are presented, as well as the respective artworks and furnishings from the nineteenth and twentieth century.

Connecting Gallery (Room 77)

Similar to Room 49, this connecting hallway was painted after the model of the Vatican Loggia. The fifteen picture fields, based on designs by Hesse and other contemporary engravings, show Italian scenes, among them Rome, Florence, Verona, and Naples. The **marble bust** of Bacchus by August Wredow from the mid-nineteenth century is part of the original furnishings. The lost pieces have been replaced by the bust of an athlete (anonymous sculptor) and a Hermes bust by Fritz Schulze.

Connecting Gallery

Red Room (Room 79)

This small room was originally an anteroom and was largely destroyed by the remodelling undertaken for the military museum. Fragments of the ceiling mouldings, the stencilled designs, and the marble fireplace have survived. When the room was renovated in 2004, the oak parquet floor was reconstructed. The **bust**, by Christian Daniel Rauch (1777–1857), depicts Frederick William IV. The **paintings** belong to the nineteenth century furnishings.

Blue Room (Room 80)

After 1850, this room served as a living room for summer guests and after 1882 it was part of the children's apartment. In his interior design around

Red Room, historical photo from the 1930s

1845, Hesse made use of older door panels and overdoors. The **marble reliefs** over the doors, by Ridolfo Schadow (1786–1822), depict two scenes from the myth of Castor and Pollux. Further scenes from this myth are to be found in picture fields in the ceiling painting. In 2004, the gilt skirting boards, the skirting panels, and the parquet floors were reconstructed. The **portraits** of Christian Daniel Rauch, Johann Gottfried Schadow, and Christian Ludwig Ideler, recipient of the order Pour le Mérite, were part of the original furnishings. The painting of Peter Cornelius is a replacement for a lost portrait from the same series. The two Minerva **statues**, by Julius Troschel, standing in the niches, were acquired for the Marble Palace in 1838. In order to complete the impression of the room as recorded in pictures, the lost **furniture** has been replaced by similar pieces.

Blue Room

Green Cabinet (Room 81)

After 1850, the Green Cabinet was used as either a writing room, a lady-in-waiting chamber, a hallway or a cabinet. After 1882, it served as a bedroom in the children's apartment. And from 1904, it was the bedroom of the nanny. The restoration of the ceiling paintings took place in 1988, and the oak parquet floors were reconstructed in 2004. The **furniture** belonged to the furnishings of the Marble Palace. Frederick William IV acquired the Romantic ruin **paintings**, landscapes, and vedute for the furnishings of the Potsdam palaces.

Living Room (Muse's Room) (Room 82)

This room was decorated as a living room in 1847, and later served as either a dining room or a bedroom. The ceiling painting shows twelve medallions with female figures. The marble fireplace and the fireplace mirror are from after 1881; the oak parquet floor is a modern reconstruction. The **paintings** by Albert Eichhorn (1811–1851) were commissioned in the mid-eighteenth century by King Frederick William IV. They depict famous buildings of Classical antiquity and previously belonged to the furnishings of the South Wing. The mahogany furniture crafted around 1790 and around 1840 were used in the Marble Palace in the nineteenth century.

Bathroom (Room 83)

This small room was refurbished as a toilet room in 1847. It was later used as a writing room, servant's room, and bathroom. Some of the original wall framings and the veneered door have survived. Part of the

Muse's Room

Pompeiian-style putti-frieze also has survived. The room was restored in 2003/05. In 1882, in the neighbouring room, called the "Retraite" in 1847, there was a "mahogany water closet".

Bedroom (Room 85)

This walls of this room, which was furnished as a bedroom in 1847, were hung with blue, flowered fabric around 1900. Largely destroyed in 1960, a simpler version was reconstructed in 2004. The gilt **furni-**

Ludwig Ferdinand Hesse, cabinet in the North Wing of the Marble Palace in Potsdam, around 1851

ture (around 1880) was in use during imperial times. Heinrich von Angeli painted the **portraits** of Prince William (II.) and Princess Auguste Viktoria. They originated in the Potsdam City Palace.

Green Living Room (Room 87)

In 1847, the walls of this room were painted green and provided with gilt skirting boards. The wall painting showing two Antique chariots (charioteers) by Bernhard Wilhelm Rosendahl and the marble fireplace have survived, and the parquet floor was reconstructed in 2004. The **paintings** and the **vases** from the Königliche Porzellan Manufaktur (KPM), display Potsdam vedute from the nineteenth century that are mostly from other palaces. The furniture was in use during imperial times. The furnishing of the Green Living Room included the mahogany **escritoire** from 1800.

Purple Room (Room 88)

After 1960, this room, which was once used as a living or sleeping room, was largely destroyed. The ceiling painting and some of the skirting boards, as well as part of the elm-wood base panel survived. The restoration of the room was finished in 2004 with the reconstruction of the parquet floor. In 1908, Philipp Alexius von László (1869–1937) painted the **portrait** of Crown Princess Cecilie, who after her marriage to Crown Prince William in 1904 resided in the Marble Palace. Her first three sons were born here and grew up in the Children's Apartment in the North Wing. Cecilie had the pear-wood **armchair** brought to the palace from Schloss Gelbensande in Mecklenburg. It remained in the Marble Palace until the royal pair

◁ Escritoire
in the Green
Living Room

△ Philipp von Lazlo,
Crown Princess Cecilie,
1908

moved into the newly constructed Schloss Cecilienhof in 1917.

Kloeber Hall (Room 95)

In 1847, this small hall was provided with an alcove
framed with plaster columns and pilasters. It served
alternately as a dining room or a bedroom. In 1845–
47, the painter of history paintings August Kloeber
created the large **wall painting** depicting mytholog-
ical and allegorical scenes. In 1854, a skylight was
built in to improve the lighting for the painting. The
main painting, which fills the whole far wall, shows
Venus rising out of the sea on a shell. On the wall with

Historical photo of Kloeber Hall, 1933

the door, across from the alcove, are Bacchus and Ariadne on the left, and on the right Apollo playing the lyre in the company of shepherds. Next to the alcove, on the right, the painting of Mercury has survived. Its counterpart on the left, which was destroyed by fire in 1944, depicted the winged Genius of Sleep. Furthermore, the door wings with their veneers with precious woods, the overdoor painting by Kloeber, the black marble fireplace, parts of the plaster cornices, some wooden panels and gilt picture frames all survived. The faux marble pillars and the parquet floor were reconstructed in 2004.

Marble Palace
Im Neuen Garten 10
14469 Potsdam
Telephone: +49(0)331.9694-550
Telefax: +49(0)331.9694-556
E-mail: marmorpalais@spsg.de

Contact
Stiftung Preußische Schlösser und Gärten
Berlin-Brandenburg
Postanschrift:
Postfach 601462
14414 Potsdam

Information at:

Besucherzentrum am Neuen Palais
Am Neuen Palais 3
14469 Potsdam

Opening Hours:
April–October: 9–6
November–March: 10–5
Closed Tuesdays

and in:

Visitor Centre at the Historic Mill
An der Orangerie 1
14469 Potsdam
Tel.: +49 (0) 331.96 94-200
Fax: +49 (0) 331.96 94-107
E-Mail: info@spsg.de

Opening Hours
April–October 8:30–5:30
November–March 8:30–4:30

Group Reservations
Tel.: +49 (0) 331.96 94-222
E-Mail: gruppenservice@spsg.de

Opening Hours and Entrance Fees
The Marble Palace is open on the weekends from November to April, and from May to October, Tuesday through Sunday.

Current opening hours and fees can be found at www.spsg.de

Near the Marble Palace is Schloss Cecilienhof, which Emperor William II had built, from 1913 to 1917, for his oldest son, Crown Prince William and his wife Crown Princess Cecilie. Alongside the palace rooms with their largely original furnishings, the palace also offers the opportunity to experience an authentic location of the historically and politically significant events of the Potsdam Conference of 1945.

Also accessible by way of a footpath are the nearby Pfingstberg, with its Belvedere, built 1847–1863 after the designs of Frederick William IV, and the Pomona Temple, designed by Karl Friedrich Schinkel in 1800. The most beautiful view in Potsdam can be enjoyed from the towers of the Belvedere.

Public Transportation
from Berlin: S1 or RE1 to Potsdam Hauptbahnhof (central station)
from Potsdam Hauptbahnhof: Bus 695, 638, 639 or 609, or Tram 92 or 96 to Reiterweg/Alleestraße, then Bus 603 to Birkenstraße
(Please check schedules in regard to possible route changes and more up-to-date schedules.)

Information for Visitors with Disabilities

The whole ground floor of the Marble Palace is barrier-free and wheelchair accessible. The upper floor of the main building is not wheelchair accessible.

Wheelchairs are available for visitors with impaired mobility. An elevator for wheelchairs and a WC with disabled access are located in the entrance area.

Further Information: handicap@spsg.de

Museum Shops

The museum shops at the Prussian Palaces and Gardens invite you to further explore the world of the kings and queens of Prussia – and to take that experience home with you. Your purchases are in fact donations, because the profits of the Museumsshop GmbH help to support the acquisition of works of art and to augment necessary restorations of the SPSG's palaces and gardens.
www.museumsshop-im-schloss.de

Gastronomy

Meierei Brauhaus im Neuen Garten
Am Neuen Garten 10
Tel.: +49(0)331.70432-12
www.meierei-potsdam.de

Tourismus-Marketing Brandenburg GmbH (TMB)
Am Neuen Markt 1
14467 Potsdam
Tel.: +49(0)331.29873-0
E-Mail: tmb@reiseland-brandenburg.de
www.reiseland-brandenburg.de

Preservation of the Historic Gardens and Their Design

The Prussian cultural landscapes in Potsdam and Berlin have been listed as UNESCO World Heritage Sites since 1990. We need your support in protecting this cultural heritage and the exceptional works of art within this fragile natural environment!

By behaving considerately, you will help to ensure that you and other visitors may continue to enjoy these historic gardens in all their splendour. The park regulations of the Stiftung Preußische Schlösser und Gärten Berlin-Brandenburg (SPSG) are designed to protect and conserve this unique heritage, and to assist you in conducting yourself appropriately and considerately.

Your observation of these regulations is greatly appreciated!

We hope you will enjoy your visit to the royal Prussian gardens.

Literature

Bissing, Wilhelm Moritz Freiherr von, *Friedrich Wilhelm II., König von Preußen*, Duncker & Humblot, Berlin 1967

Sichelschmidt, Gustav, Friedrich Wilhelm II. *Der »Vielgeliebte« und seine galante Zeit* Eine Biographie, VGB-Verlagsgesellschaft Berg, Berg am See 1993

Friedrich Wilhelm II. und die Künste. Preußens Weg zum Klassizismus. Ausstellungskatalog der SPSG, Potsdam 1997

Neumann, Hans-Joachim, Friedrich Wilhelm II. *Preußen unter den Rosenkreuzern*, edition q, Berlin 1997

Quilitzsch, Uwe, Wedgwood. *Klassizistische Keramik in den Gärten der Aufklärung*, L+H Verlag, Berlin 1997

Bringmann, Wilhelm, *Preußen unter Friedrich Wilhelm II. (1786–1797)*, P. Lang, Frankfurt am Main-Berlin-Bern-Bruxelles-New York-Oxford-Wien 2001

Otte, Wilma, *Das Marmorpalais. Ein Refugium am Heiligen See*, Prestel-Verlag, München-Berlin-London-New York 2003

Meier, Brigitte, *Friedrich Wilhelm II. – König von Preußen (1744–1797). Ein Leben zwischen Rokoko und Revolution.* Verlag Friedrich Pustet, Regensburg 2007

Hagemann, Alfred P., Wilhelmine von Lichtenau (1753–1820). *Von der Mätresse zur Mäzenin*, Böhlau Verlag, Köln Weimar Wien 2007

Otto, Karl-Heinz, *Friedrich Wilhelm II. König im Schatten Friedrichs des Großen*, Kulturhistorischer Führer in Wort und Bild, Edition Märkische Reisebilder, Potsdam 2008

Otto, Karl-Heinz, *Gräfin Lichtenau. Mätresse und Lebensliebe Friedrich Wilhelms II.*, Kulturhistorischer Führer in Wort und Bild, Edition Märkische Reisebilder, Potsdam 2009

Photos

Photos: PhoBildarchiv SPSG/Photographers: Wolfgang Pfauder (pp. 6, 8, 12–14, 16–18, 20–21, 26, 33, 35, 38–39, back cover), Leo Seidel (pp. 7, 10, 29, 31, 40), Daniel Lindner (pp. 2/3, 22/23), Roland Handrick (front cover inside flap, pp. 9, 27), Hans Bach (front cover, p. 1), Hagen Immel (p. 28)
Maps: SPSG/Editor: Beate Laus

Imprint

Published by the Stiftung Preußische Schlösser und Gärten Berlin-Brandenburg (SPSG)
Text: Stefan Gehlen
Editing (German): Jana Krassa
Proof-reading: Barbara Grahlmann
English translation: Catherine Framm
Layout: Hendrik Bäßler, Berlin
Coordination: Elvira Kühn
Printing: DZA Druckerei zu Altenburg GmbH, Altenburg

The Deutsche Nationalbibliothek (German National Library) lists this publication in the Deutsche Nationalbibliografie; detailed bibliographic data are available on the Internet: http://dnb.d-nb.de.

© 2020 Stiftung Preußische Schlösser und Gärten Berlin-Brandenburg, Deutscher Kunstverlag GmbH Berlin Munich
ISBN 978-3-422-98309-0